AF484489

Power
Confidence
Ambition
Drive
Sunshine
Cheerful
Manipura
Identity

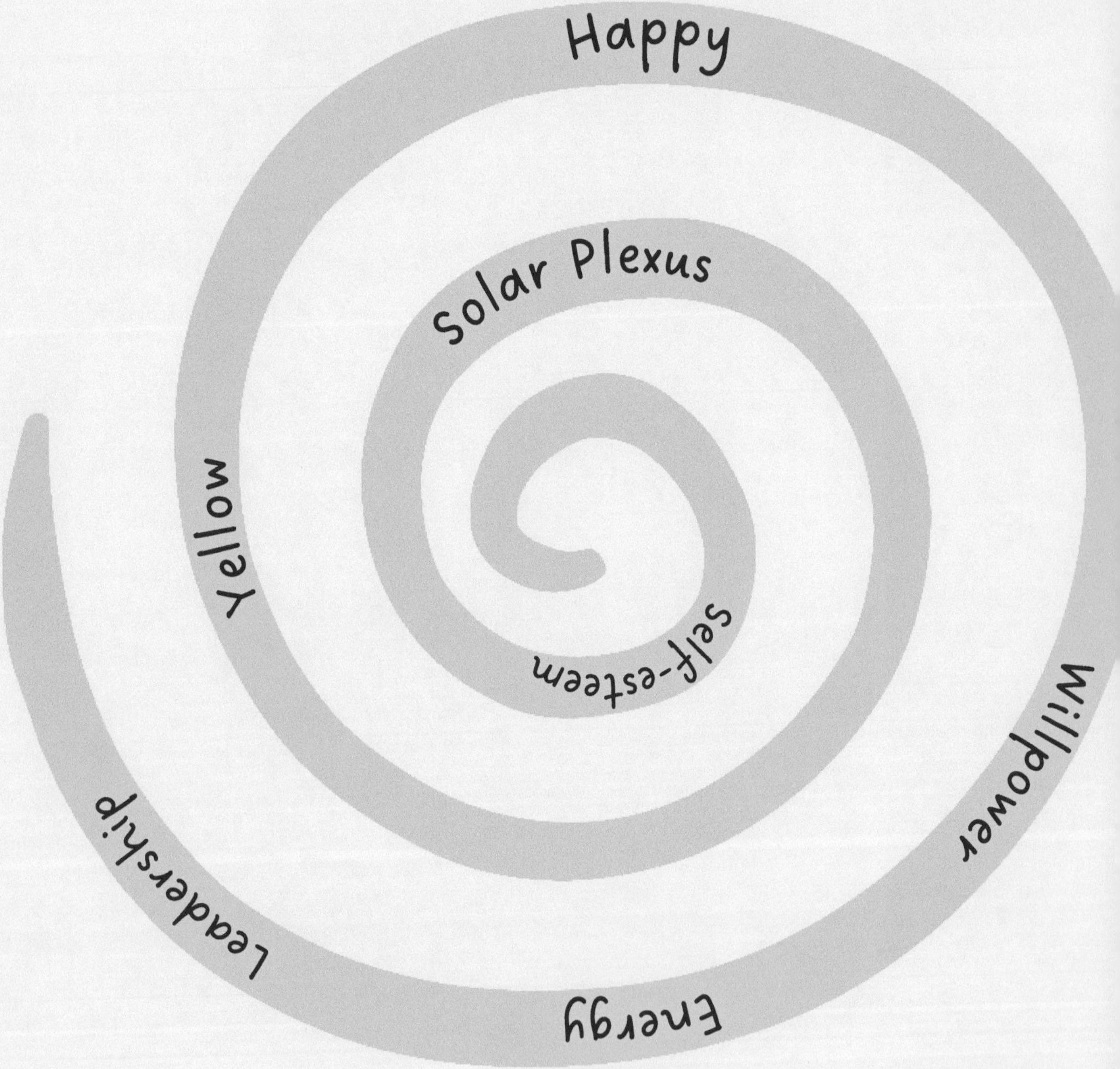

Happy
Solar Plexus
Yellow
Self-esteem
Willpower
Energy
Leadership

Solar Plexus Chakra Adventures:

Shining Bright

with

Sunny and Sphen

Volume 3

By: K.C. Gold

*"This book is dedicated to you.
Stand up for what you believe in."*

Northern Lights Publishing LLC.

https://northernlightskids.com/

Greetings, I'm Sunny,
With Sphen by my side,
We are spinning energy particles
Where your courage and strength reside.

Sphen, look at that treehouse!
Yeah, it looks like fun, but it's so high up.

We swirl around your
tummy,
We have a yellow glow,
Sometimes they call us Solar
Plexus Chakra,
And we love to help you
grow.

We are the energy force
That helps your dreams take flight,
Confidence, energy, and self-esteem
Are all our allies.

We love to have fun
And assist you too,
But sometimes, a helping
hand from you is due.

"There's nothing I can do."

If ever you feel powerless,

Or
unsure
what to do,

It signals a
blockage
is within you.

There are ways to get us

spinning, yes, it is true,

Back to 528 times, plus two.

100Hz
200Hz
300Hz
400Hz
500Hz
600Hz
700Hz
800Hz
900Hz
1000Hz
1100Hz
1200Hz
Hertz Meter
1 Hertz (Hz) = 1 Spin Per Second
528Hz

Sweet sounds are delightful,
'E' is our favorite note,
With its pitch so bright,
Our spin will start to float.

Dance to your favorite song,
let your tummy groove,
Feel us swirl and twirl with
every move.

Feast on yellow treasures,
Pineapples and lemons are a delight,
And let their vibrant energy fill you with sweet light.

Dress in our color, something yellow, happy, and bright, Pretty soon you will feel the warmth and the glow of its sunlight.

Try sitting in a quiet place,
anywhere will do,
And once you are calm and
focused, repeat a mantra
that speaks to you:

"Obstacles come, yet
with solar plexus
power,
I rise tall and conquer
them all."

"I am brave, I am bright, like a firework lighting up the night."

"In control of my actions, my response is the key

To creating positive change just for me."

"Motivated by the sun's warm embrace, I chase my dreams with a smile on my face."

A yellow sun shines in your belly's hold,
Filling you with courage, daring, and bold.

With confidence rising, you face challenges bright, Solar Plexus Chakra, your guiding light.

SUPER HEROES
Drive
Confidence
Willpower
Courage
Yes, we did it!
This is so much fun!

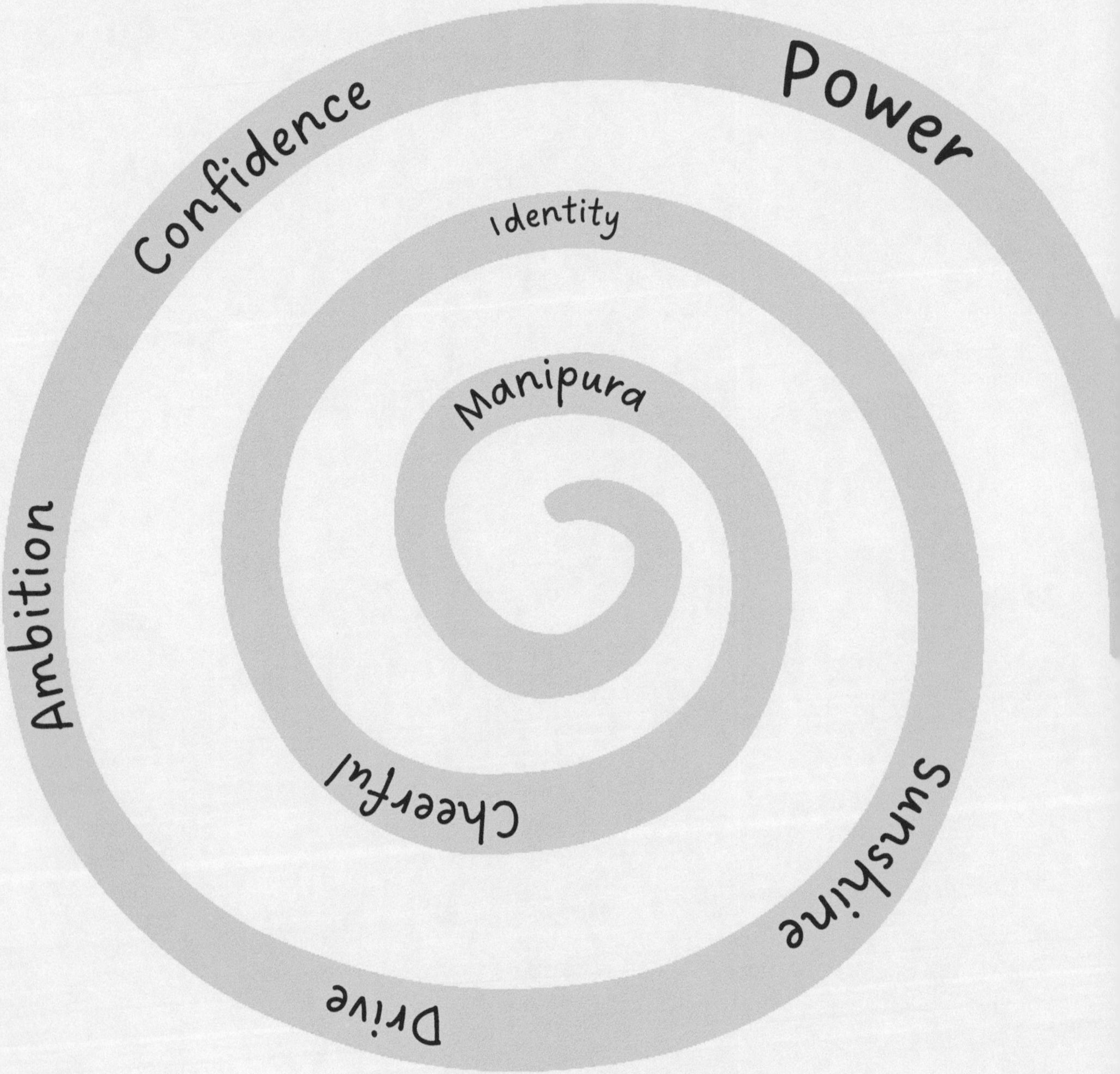

Power
Confidence
Identity
Manipura
Ambition
Cheerful
Drive
Sunshine

Dear Reader,

Thank you for taking the time to read this book. If you found value in it, I would be incredibly grateful if you could take a few moments to leave a review. Your feedback not only helps me improve but also aids other readers in discovering books they might enjoy.

Thank you once again for your support and for being a part of this adventure!

Warm regards,
K.C. Gold

Amazon

Northern Lights
Publishing

Stand up for what you believe in.